UNWOVEN THOUGHTS

POEMS

IBBY

Made with ♥ on the Notion Press Platform
www.notionpress.com

"To my dreams, my doubts, and the messy, beautiful moments in between.
To the friends who've shared their laughter and their tears,
To the quiet corners where I've found myself,
And to the ones who told me my voice mattered when I wasn't sure.

This book is for anyone who's ever felt too much, too little, or just not enough.
May these words remind you that you're never truly alone.
Here's to finding strength in the mess, and magic in the chaos."

Contents

Contents

Contents

Contents

Foreword

Dear reader,

In the delicate spaces between words, there exists a world of emotion, truth, and discovery. Poetry is the art of capturing these fleeting moments, of weaving them into something eternal and yet profoundly intimate. As you turn the pages of this collection, you will be invited into a landscape of thought and feeling, where each line speaks not only to the heart, but also to the soul.

This book is a journey through the quiet yet powerful language of the human experience. The poems within reflect both the universal and the deeply personal — the joy of new beginnings, the ache of loss, the beauty of fleeting moments, and the endless search for meaning. It is a reflection of the intricacies of life, expressed through the simplicity and complexity of verse.

As you read, I encourage you to allow the rhythm of the words to guide you, to savor the weight of silence between the lines, and to embrace the power of poetry to unearth the truths we often overlook. May these poems resonate with you, spark your own reflections, and remind you of the boundless beauty of language.

Welcome to a journey that begins with a single line, but will stay with you long after the last word is read.

Preface

In the quiet spaces between words, I have found fragments of myself—pieces of the past, echoes of dreams, and whispers of the world around me. This collection of poems,Unwoven Thoughts , is a journey through those moments, each verse an attempt to capture the fleeting, elusive beauty of life in its many forms.

I've always believed that poetry has a way of making the intangible feel real—of giving voice to the thoughts and emotions we often struggle to articulate. These poems are born from the complexities of human experience, from joy and sorrow to love and loss. They are a reflection of the quiet contemplations and loud questions that surface in the stillness of everyday life.

As you turn these pages, I invite you to explore the landscapes of emotion, thought, and experience within these verses. May they resonate with you in ways that words alone cannot explain, and may they remind you of the quiet power of poetry to illuminate our lives.

"*With gratitude and hope,*

Basheera Fatima"

Acknowledgements

I would like to express my deepest gratitude to all those who have supported me in the creation of this poetry book. This journey would not have been possible without the love, encouragement, and inspiration I have received from so many.

To my family, thank you for your unwavering belief in me. Your love and patience have been my foundation, and your support has allowed me to chase my dreams fearlessly. I am eternally grateful for each of you.

To my friends, thank you for your kindness, laughter, and the beautiful conversations that sparked many of my poems. You have all played a part in shaping my thoughts and creativity, and I'm so thankful for each of you.

Lastly, I would like to thank myself for having the courage to express my thoughts, dreams, and emotions through poetry. Writing has been both a refuge and a celebration, and this book is a piece of my heart, shared with all of you.

> "*This book is a reflection of my experiences, my thoughts, and my heart. I hope it resonates with you as much as it does with me.*"

Prologue

In the quiet moments between the noise of everyday life, poetry has always been my refuge—a place where I could unravel thoughts, confront feelings, and make sense of the world around me. This collection is a reflection of that journey, a gathering of moments both big and small, filled with joys, sorrows, dreams, and reflections. Each poem is a piece of my heart, an honest expression of who I am, and where I have been.

Through these pages, I invite you to walk with me on a path paved with words. Some of these poems were born from the beauty of fleeting moments, while others emerged from the depths of struggles and uncertainties. But in every line, there is truth—a truth that I hope resonates with you, the reader, as deeply as it does with me.

Poetry, for me, is not just about writing; it's about listening. It's about paying attention to the subtle whispers of the world around us—the ones that often go unnoticed. And in these quiet whispers, I have found stories worth telling.

> *"So, as you turn these pages, I ask you to listen too. Listen to the rhythm of life, to the echoes of the heart, and to the stories within you waiting to be heard. This book is as much yours as it is mine. With every word, I hope you find a reflection of yourself in the spaces between the verses."*

1. Not a word....

No one to speak in silence,
Does it mean it's going to be silence,
The word itself speaks it's meaning,
So quiet and calm , it's appealing
It takes years to speak in silence ,
Beacause it's always quiet.
No one to bother for a word,
I think they might take sword.
Paper tearing to bits and bits ,
In the silence of seas.
Blowing away or reaching out,
The perfect way to get out.
Sitting in a chair idle ,
And blowing the last candle .
Just dreaming in my own world ,
Beacause I don't want to be heard .
No one to speak in silence ,
Does it mean it's going to be quiet

2. Beauty of the Earth

Light pink pale sunshine
Soften that moon line
Light so bright can't see your flying kite
Love to see high up in the sky
In the corner with some evening pie
So soothing sound as sweetness fell on the ground
Coming across and meets the sea
Feel like having fritters and tea
So warm but still chilly!
Come on it's snowing silly
Building up the best snowman
Frying up some eggs in pan
Flowers blooming all around
Collecting it or it will be blown

3. Other Side

The blank reflection I see,
In the wavy of nothingness
I see what I do
Not the mirror knowing my next move
Passing by to see the future
Of catepillars crawling on my shoulders
Thinking about all the lies
Going inside dimensions, i sigh
What if it's real in the other side
The opposite of the fights
If only I could explore
And find the mirrors's core
What if colors aren't bright
And things aren't out of sight
What if people aren't alike
And buildings aren't what I see
Imaginable things an't be real
If I could just make a deal
Water could be air, people - sand
If i could just outstrech a hand
Talking to myself not wanting to shout
The way mirror got a cut
Smashing every glass to get an answer

How to , when to , what to
As I was thining a voice called me
As it was crawling by my side
As i looked upon I couldn't believe my eyes
As i saw what I imagined in the laughing cries
And then the little one
Called me in a corner and said
'It's real if you wish it's stupid if you don't believe"
As I was about to scream
I woke up and thought " it's just a dream"

4. If I were you

Watching clouds cry above
The sound it makes that I adore
It feels like so soothing inside
Like an angel sat beside
The rain is a description of me
Just like after anger gaze
I cry to let the pain out
Maybe the rain copies my act out
People love rain as it pleasing to see
But my thought is to know how it actually feels
Drop by drop , I collect the tears
Not knowing where it has dissappears
Blowing trees, and houses
Starts like a teardrop
But then it never stops
Rain speaks to me, it tells me it's story
by far the most dreadful one cry I have heard so far
I personify it as a person who is lot
and wanting to escape from those gloomy angry clouds
The tears falling drip by drip
Rain is in every person, maybe not visible to every eye
As tears can be mistaken with those happy myths
Usually hiding it to get away

That one person catches you who knows your story

5. School Days

When school days fade and summers here to stay
I bid farewell to classrooms and a world of dismay
no more walking early no more howeworks plight
I am free to roam and shared the memories I have enjoyed
I will cherish memories of friends and the laughter we shared
of all lessons learned and moments that will never be
impaired
the thrill of discovery the joy of growth and play
will stay with me forever come what may
I will take with me skills and the knowledge I have gained
to face the world ahead with confidence and no strain
I will imagine to shape my own way
and make a difference come what may
So here is to the future and all it's unknown might
I will face with courage and a heart full of light
for though I leave school behind I will stay
And the memories we have made and the lessons we have
learned each day

6. Beauty of the sky

Oh! The beauty of the sky , so high and bright
A canvas painted with colors of delight
The sun a masterpiece of golden light
Paints the clouds with hues of blue and white
The sky a work of art so fine fair
A reflection of that's just still there
The stars like diamond in the night
Twinkle with grace a celestial sight
The moon a glowing orb silver light
Illuminates the path a beacon bright
The clouds like puffs of cotton candy
Dance and frolic a wondrous sight to see
The sky a symphony of color and light
A masterpiece of nature a true delight
A source of inspiration a place of peace
A beauty that never ceases to release

7. (A Quiet Place)

In a quiet place here the world slows down
I find peace my heart and soul profound
The trees stands tall , their leaves rustle and sway
A gentle breeze whispers through the day
In the quiet place I find my heaven
A refuge from the world a place to be given
A place to dream a place to heal
A place to find my peace heart's reveal

8. OVERTHINKING

Oh! the weight of thought that plague my mind
overthinking a curse I can't unwind
Ever decision a mountain to climb
The fear of failure a constant refrain
In the depths of my soul storm brews
Torrential thoughts a never- ending hue
I am lost in a sea of " what if " and " maybes"
Drowning in a sea of self - doubt and sighs
The gears of mind they never cease
A never - ending cycle of anxiety and freeze
I am trapped in a maze with no escaape
The walls of my mind they never break
Oh! how I wish for a peaeful mind
Free from the chains of overthinking I would be kind
But alas it's a burden I cannot shake
A heavy load a constant heartbreak
So I will wander in my own thoughts
A prisoner of my own overthinking , I have been caught
But maybe just maybe I will find a way
To break free from this cycle come what may

9. Imaginative world beyond ......

In the worlds beyond our own where dreams take flight
A realm of wonder where the imaginative reigns begin
Where the trees are made of candy cane and the skies are painted with glee
In this world of enchantment all hinges are possible to see
The creatures that roam are a sight to behold
From dragons to unicorns to behold
Their scales shimmer in the sun their wings take to the air
In this world of magic no creature is beyond compare
The river run with chocolate and the mountain made of cake
In this world of sweetness no one ever has to break
The flowers bloom in every hue
In this world all is well you will see
So come and visit and don't be shy
In this world of imagination the sky is high
For in this world beyond our own dreams we hold dear
are the ones that bring us near

10. Changing The Past

In dreams , I see a path not taken
A chance missed a moment unspoken
The what , it's and the maybes
Haunt me like a ghostly presence
I long to turn back time
To seize the day to make mine
To change the course of history
And alter the present's design
But the part it holds me tight
A reminder of what's not right
A burden I cannot shake
A longing that will never break

11. To Myself

When I am alone I find peace
Like a calm sea a soul releases
From the waves of thoughts my mind does cease
And in the silence I find peace
In this quiet place I hear my heart
It whispers secrets and shares it's art
I am free to be , to dream, to roam
To change my passions to make my home
So here i will stay in this peaceful nest
And let my heart guide me and be at rest
For in the stillness I make it best
And in my silence I fond my quest
Amidst the whispers of the mind
A voice calls out a gentle find
Within the depths of heart and soul
A quest for self discovery of whole
The mirror's reflection , clear and true
Reveals the beauty pure and new
The strength of spirit unbroken and strong
A self - potrait forever young
The beauty of self so bold
Shines like a star forever to be told
The journey within a path so true

Leads to a love for self forever new

12. ~EMPTINESS~

In the void I find my peace
A silence that my soul can seize
The world outside may be din
But in my heart I am within
The echoes of the past fade slow
As I let go of all that flow
The weight of emptiness of memories , the pain
I leave it all and walk again
The emptiness that one seemed gray
Now shines with light a bright way
To find myself to let go free
And be the me that's meant to be

13. *Getting lost in a book*

In the pages I wonder I lost my way
In the world of words I stray
The stories they weave a magic spell
In the depths of a book I find my home
Where the characters roam
Their lives and love , their trails strife
Become my own precious life
The lines and words , a symphony
A world of dreams for me to see
I escape in the book's embrace
And find my heart's place
In the quiet of a page, I find my voice
A word of my own a joyous noise
The words and rhymes what a choice
I am lost but Oh! so free

14. .....WISHES.....

The situation of the heart needs peace
every wish needs to be fulfilled
the way earlier there was
no need to wish for anything
why do I want it the same again
The heart wants the feeling of
your being there in such a way
that it wants you day and night
you are wanted , everytime
Why don't I want anyone elses
other than you
In every journey I want you as a guide
To live , I just need you !

15. Feeling ALIVE

In the depths of my soul
Awakening with each breath
A spark ignites a fire within
Embracing the present moment
Savouring each sensation
The rush of adrenaline
Pulses through my veins
I am alive
In this enchanting world
Where the moon kissed the sky
And the wind touched my cheeks
My heart beats with purpose
Every beat a reminder
Of the gift of being alive
In this vast beautiful universe

16. t o r n

a heart once whole now frayed at the seams
pulled in two directions , unraveling dreams
love whispers sweetly , yet doubts start to creep
in the shadows of chaos ,where silence runs deep
promises scattered like leaves in the breeze
each breeze of word is of a painful unease
the mirror reflects a jumbled facade
a potrait of longing of hope and scars
fingers tracing paths of the past's bitter thread
with every soft echo the mind spins like a lead
yet, in the torn edges there's beauty to find
a resiliance flickers a light intertwined
for every split moment that breaks me apart
is a chance to rebuild to ignite a new start
is a chance to gather the pieces though jagged and worn
embracing the journey of being beautifully torn...

17. Hope

Hope is a whisper in the darkest night,
A flicker of warmth, a guiding light.
It's the breath that stirs when all seems still,
A quiet promise, a quiet will.
When shadows fall and doubts arise,
Hope lifts the heart, it clears the skies.
Like dawn that breaks through midnight's shade,
Hope's gentle hand will never fade.
It is the strength we don't always see,
A hidden current, wild and free.
It's the courage to rise, though we've been torn,
The belief that something new is born.
In the midst of storms, in moments of pain,
Hope is the rainbow after the rain.
It whispers softly, "You are not alone,"
It plants the seed, it starts to grow.
It's the dream that dances when all seems lost,
The spark that burns despite the cost.
It's the belief that we'll find our way,
That brighter skies will greet the day.
So hold on tight, don't let it go,
For hope will lead you, this you know.
In every trial, in every fight,

Hope is the flame that guides the night.

18. DEADLY DISCOVERY !!

Beneath the rusted bridge
where shadows lurk and whispers
slide a patch of earth stirs
hidden treasures of the past
unearthed by careless feet on carefree day
A glint catches the eye
nothing more than jagged piece of metal
but rise from the ground
the echoes of long last memories
victories and sorrows buried deep
their stories woven into thier sacred soils
With a rush of wind the air thickens
a warning hanging like autumn leaves
the past rustles in the underbush revealing truth that breathes
yet threathes to choke
A child's laughter hangs heavy farmed in the roots of the darkening trees
while the heavy pulse of history beats
against tender hearts reminding; not all discoveries
fill with joy or leave you unchanged
Hands tremble at the edges of knowing
minds spin in a dance of dread and wonder

what was it lingered here
a deadly whispers , a take untold where
curiosity tiptoes and innocence unravels

19. bitterSweet

Turning happiness into frowns
With jsut a few words
It's like a storm that comes
And leaves the sky blurred
A smile replaced with tears
Joy replaced with sorrow
The pain cuts deep like spears
Leaving no hope tomorrow
Words can hurt more than sticks
Leaving wounds that are deep
Turning laughter into kicks
And stealing away your sleep
But through it all , we are strong
And rise above the hate
For happiness will soon belong
To those who chooses love not fate

20. F.R.I.E.N.D.S

Through there is gold up in the moutain lovely pearls deep in the sea
those treasures do not mean as much as your friendship means to me
while diamonds may be beautiful and worth a lot of money
they cannot give a warm embrace or share jokes we think are funny
knowing that I have had your friendship will be a treasured memory
Best friends stick together till the end
they are like a straight line that will never bend
they trust each other forever
no matter if they are apart or together
they help you up when you fall
your true friends will have your back , as they are best of all

21. the art of waiting.....

Patience , oh! so virtue so rare
A quality beyond compare
To wait with grace to endure
A test of character for sure
In times of trial a steady hand
To navigate life's shifting sand
To trust in the journey's pace
And find solace in the god's embrace
Patience , well of inner strength
A guiding light of boundless length
To temper anger , soften strife
And embrace the rhythm of life
So let's cultivate this gift
In moments of tension , let it lift
Our hearts to a place of peace
And in patience , find release

22. Were ur' ears ringing ?

Your worth is not defined by other's worth
it's a truth that you alone can choose
your value shines from within
unaffected by the world's din
Stand tall, embrace your unique self
let not their judgements sit on the shelf
your path is yours to forge and explore
unbound by what was aid before
Believe in the strength that passes
for your worth is not for them to assess
walk forward with confidence and grace
your light will always find it's place

23. The convey of life

The convey of life has stopped at strange place
we had gone to find solace , but ended up losing sleep
the path we thought was clear now shrouded in a haze
leaving us to wander our hearts heavy and deep
the family landmarks have faded from view
replaced by a landscape that is foreign and cold
we search for the comfort we once knew
but the answers we seek remain untold
the silence is deafening the air thick with unease
as we try to make sense of this unexpected turn
the jouney we embarked on no longer at ease
leaving us to wonder what lessons we must learn
yet , In the midst of this strange and unsettling place
we find a glimmer of hope a spark that refuges to die
for within the darkness we may yet find grace
and the strength to carry on as the convey of life goes by....

24. ....

In life's fleeting dance we tread with uncertainities head but
when it's time to say goodbye let's do it with a smile not a sigh
for we cannot control our fate but we can choose how we
relate to the end that waits how we relate lt's embrace it ,
stand tall in our final moments let's show grace let love and
kindness take it's place for in death's embrace we find the
beauty of a life well - aligned
so let's face our end with grace and leave behind a lasting
trace of joy and goodwill in every mile and when it's time ,
let's die with a smile .

25. Solitary

In the quiet of world unspoken,
Solitude wraps its arms, unbroken.
A gentle sigh, a whispered plea,
A soul adrift in deep still sea.
No voices call, no laughter rings,
Just the hum of time's soft wings.
The heart, a bird within its cage,
Turns its thoughts to every age.
In the silence, echoes speak,
Of dreams once bold, now quiet and weak.
Yet in this calm, a spark is found,
A peace that builds without a sound.
Solitude, though often feared,
Can teach the soul that's long adhered
To noise and crowd, to ceaseless race,
That stillness holds a sacred space.
For in this quiet, there is growth,
A chance to heal, to learn, to both
Embrace the self, the truth inside,
No need for masks, no need to hide.
So solitude, a gift so pure,
In its embrace, we are secure.
For sometimes, silence is the key,

To unlocking all we're meant to be.

26. The Night Sky

Beneath the velvet curtain high,
A thousand stars adorn the sky,
Whispers of the moonlight dance,
In silent waves, a cosmic trance.
The constellations paint their tales,
Of ancient gods and windswept sails,
Each twinkling light a story told,
In silver threads of space and gold.
The night, a canvas vast and deep,
Where dreams and mysteries softly sleep,
And in the stillness, hearts may find,
The endless wonder of the mind.
As shadows stretch and winds grow light,
The world below sleeps through the night,
While up above, the heavens shine,
A timeless spark, a grand design.

27. Let it be...

Burn this world to the ground with your words
let the flames of truth rise and be heard
for in the end, we all must cease to exist
so why not blaze bright before we cease and desist
Let your word spark a fire that ca't be contained
let it burn through the darkness, unashamed
for in the destruction , there can be creation
a rebirth from the ashes of civilization
So embrace the fire that burns within
let it consume you , let it begin
for in the end we all are destined to fade
so let your words be the legacy you have made

28. curiosity

Curiosity, a spark within,
A flame that stirs where dreams begin.
It whispers soft, then calls aloud,
A voice that lifts, a force unbowed.
It leads us to the unknown shore,
To places where we've not been before.
Through every question, every quest,
It seeks the truth, it will not rest.
It dances in the mind's embrace,
A longing for the hidden place.
Where answers lie in mystery,
And every turn's a new story.
Curiosity, a boundless sky,
A reason to ask, to wonder why.
With eyes wide open, hearts untamed,
We chase the knowledge, never shamed.
For in its depth, we find our grace,
A journey marked by time and space.
Curiosity, a faithful friend,
That leads us forward, without end.
Curiosity, a spark in the dark,
A flicker that grows, ignites the heart.
It pulls us forward, wide-eyed, bold,

To seek the stories yet untold.
A question asked, a mystery sought,
In every corner, wonder's caught.
With every "why" and "how" we roam,
We turn the world into our home.
It lifts the veil, it clears the mist,
Shows us the things we've long since missed.
In quiet moments, it whispers near,
"Look closer still, the truth is here."
A thirst that quenches yet never ends,
A search for answers, around each bend.
Curiosity, a restless stream,
That flows through life, a constant dream.
So let us follow, let us explore,
The endless world, the endless lore.
For in the asking, we are free,
Curiosity, our guide to be.

29. GRACIOUS

Gracious , a word that holds such power
Embodying kindness , a gentle shower
A spirit hat shines , a heart that's true
Radiating warmth , in all that you do
Gracious in thought, gracious in deed
Lifting others up , when they are in need
A guiding light , a beacon of hope
Helping us navigate life's endless scope
Gracious in manner , gracious in speech
Bringing comfort and solace , within reach
A gentle presence,a calming embrace
Gracing the world with your radiant grace
Gracious a virtue to be cherished and held
A testament to the beauty that can be unveiled
May your example inspire us all to be
Gracious in heart, mind and spirit eternally

30. Am I introverted?

In the quiet depths of my mind
I find solace in solitude
A world within myself I find
Where peace and calm exude
Away from the chaos and noise
I retreat into my own space
Where introspection brings me poise
And allows my thought to grace
I maynot seek the spotlight bright
Or crave the company of the crowd
But in my silence , I find my light
And in my solitude, I am proud
I may be introverted , it's true
But within me lies a universe
Where dreams and visions come anew
And my soul finds eternal verse

31. Between Dreams

Dreams are whispers in the silent night,
A dance of stars, a soft, ethreal light.
They carry us to places far away,
Worlds unknown in shadows lay.
In dreams, we fly on wings so wide,
Through velvet skies, on winds that glide.
We touch the moon, we kiss the sun,
And race the dawn before it's done.
They paint our hearts with colors bright,
Bring hope to dark, and calm to fright.
In every dream, a truth is found,
A secret wish, a sacred sound.
For dreams are not just visions sweet,
But roads that wind where hearts may meet.
A map to who we are inside,
A path where every soul can glide.
So dream, and dream with open eyes,
For in each dream, a future lies.
A world to shape, a chance to take
A chance to love , to live and take

32. whispers of memory

Memory is a fleeting light,
A shadow softly held in sight.
It dances in the corners deep,
A secret we are meant to keep.
Each moment lived, each word we say,
Becomes a thread that winds its way,
Through time's own tapestry, entwined,
A picture left within the mind.
Some memories are bright as gold,
Others soft and faintly bold,
Yet all of them, a part we are,
Like distant dreams, like the first star.
They live in echoes, gentle calls,
In laughter shared and silent falls.
In places we may never tread,
And faces we may never shed.
For memory, though it may fade,
Leaves behind a quiet trace,
A map that guides us through the years,
A treasure born of smiles and tears.
So hold each memory with care,
For in them all, we're always there.

Memory is a quiet stream,
A river flowing through our dreams,
It carries moments, soft and true,
And whispers tales of me and you.
It weaves its threads through time's embrace,
A patchwork quilt, a tender place,
Where faces linger, moments stay,
Even as they fade away.
Some memories are clear and bright,
Like stars that twinkle through the night,
While others are a gentle haze,
A fading glow of distant days.
Yet all of them, both light and shade,
Are pieces of the paths we've made,
A story told in silent ways,
In heartbeats, smiles, and quiet praise.
For memory is not just past,
But moments that forever last,
A bridge between the now and then,
A treasure that we hold again.
And though the years may come and go,
In memory, we always know,
That every moment we have lived,
Is a gift that time has yet to give.

33. FEAR!

Fear is a shadow, creeping low,
A whisper that makes the cold winds blow,
It twists the mind, it locks the chest,
A silent scream that won't let rest.
It wears a face you cannot see,
A fleeting thought that won't let be,
A tightening grip, a clenched-up heart,
A trembling voicc that falls apart.
It feeds on doubts, it stirs the dark,
It leaves its mark, a silent spark,
A fire that burns with no relief,
A storm inside, a quiet thief.
But fear is not the end, you see,
It's just a ghost, a fleeting plea.
For when we face it, hand in hand,
We find the strength to understand.
That fear may come, but it shall go,
It's not the master we must know,
For courage grows when we stand tall,
And rise above it, through it all.
It's eyes that watch from shadows deep,
A waking nightmare, no release,
A trembling hand, a heart that shakes,

A fear that claws, and never breaks.
The world tilts sideways, cracks and tears,
Reality shatters, no one cares,
The air is thick, the light is gone,
A scream that rises, yet it's drawn.
It holds you close, but never near,
A cold embrace, it feeds on fear,
A storm inside, a force unkind,
It takes the soul, it steals the mind.

34. CONVERSATIONS

Words weave between us like threads of light,
Silent pauses, then a spark ignites.
A gentle dance, a soft exchange,
Ideas meet, they shift, they change.
In silence, too, the messages fly,
Unspoken thoughts that never die.
A glance, a gesture, a knowing smile,
A language that transcends the mile.
We share our dreams, our fears, our truths,
In gentle tones, in laughter's proof.
Through every pause and every sound,
Connections grow, our souls unbound.
A conversation can heal, can grow,
Can help us understand and know,
That in this space, we're not alone,
In every word, we find a home.
So let us talk, let us engage,
And turn each moment into a page.
For in these talks, we truly find,
The ties that bind us, heart and mind.

35. when day becomes night

When day becomes the quiet night,
The sky unfurls its cloak of light,
Soft whispers kiss the fading sun,
And shadows stretch, the day is done.
The gold of dusk begins to fade,
As stars awake from light's cascade,
A velvet hush, a cooling air,
The world exhales, as night draws near.
The colors bleed to darker hues,
As dreams emerge, the earth renews,
The moon ascends with silver glow,
While sleepy rivers gently flow.
The sun retreats, its journey through,
And in its place, the stars anew,
The quiet hum of night's embrace,
A calm that fills the empty space.
In this transition, still and slow,
The world slips deep, the night to know,
And as the day lets go its light,
We find our peace in soft twilight.

36. is it real?

In a world where suns arise at night,
And shadows gleam with radiant light,
The oceans rise to kiss the sky,
And trees take root where clouds pass by.
The mountains bow, the valleys soar,
The wind stands still, but waves will roar,
The birds walk gently on the ground,
While silent whispers make no sound.
The rivers run in backward streams,
The stars are born of earthly dreams,
The earth spins slow, the moon flies fast,
And time unravels, never lasts.
In this world of opposites bold,
Where warmth is frozen, and ice is gold,
Laughter echoes in the dark,
And silence leaves a constant spark.
Yet in this world, we'd still survive,
For even here, we'd feel alive,
A place of change, of odd delight,
Where wrong is right, and day is night.

37. REFLECTIONS

Reflections dance on still waters deep,
A mirror of the thoughts we keep.
In every ripple, a story lies,
A glimpse of truth, a soft disguise.
The world we see, both near and far,
Is shaped by how we view the star.
In quiet moments, we take the time,
To look within, to seek, to climb.
A glance at past, a fleeting face,
The echoes of a long-lost trace.
Reflections speak, they softly call,
A silent answer to it all.
We search for meaning in their glow,
A guide through paths we do not know.
Each image forms a whispered sound,
A mirror where our souls are found.
So in the glass, in light and shade,
We find the truth we've long delayed.
Reflections show both light and dark,
But also where we leave our mark.

38. black AND white

Black and white, a world of grace,
Two colors in a timeless space.
One, the night with shadows deep,
The other, dawn's soft light to keep.
Black is mystery, calm, and bold,
A quiet strength, a story told.
It holds the silence, wraps the air,
A place where secrets gently stare.
White is purity, bright and clear,
A canvas wide, devoid of fear.
It sings of peace, of light and day,
Where every dream can find its way.
Together, they create the dance,
A balance found in every glance.
From dark to light, from night to dawn,
In black and white, we both are drawn.
For in this world of stark contrast,
We find the depth that makes us last.
A world of shades, both pure and true,
In black and white, we see anew.
Black and white, in quiet grace,
A world of balance, a steady pace.
One holds the night, a silent shade,

The other, light, where dreams are laid.
Black is depth, where shadows play,
A mystery that hides away.
It speaks in whispers, soft and clear,
A space for thoughts to disappear.
White is fresh, a blank design,
A canvas pure, a place to shine.
It's morning's glow, the sun's first rise,
A truth reflected in clear skies.
Together they create the scene,
Where light and dark are both serene.
No good without the dark of night,
No clarity without the light.
In black and white, the world's complete,
A dance of opposites, so sweet.
In every shade, a story's told,
A harmony in contrasts bold.

39. Taste the rainbow

Taste the rainbow, let it fly,
A burst of colors in the sky.
With every hue, a flavor's born,
A sweet sensation, freshly worn.
The reds are cherries, bold and sweet,
The oranges, citrus, fresh to eat.
Yellow's honey, smooth and bright,
Like summer's sun, a pure delight.
Green's a zest of mint or lime,
A burst of freshness, so sublime.
Blueberry's calm in indigo,
A cool and quiet, gentle flow.
Purple's rich with berries' grace,
A velvet touch, a soft embrace.
Together mixed, they swirl and blend,
A rainbow's joy that has no end.
Taste the rainbow, feel it burst,
In every flavor, quench your thirst.
For in each color, life's refrain,
A world of joy, beyond the rain.

40. Never Again

Never again shall shadows creep,
Where hope was lost, where hearts did weep.
The silent tears that stained the night,
Shall vanish now, consumed by light.
Never again shall fear take hold,
Or futures dim, or dreams turn cold.
For in the dawn, the promise gleams,
A life reborn, a world of dreams.
Never again shall doubts remain,
No more to wade through endless pain.
For strength is found in every scar,
And courage born from battles far.
Never again shall we look back,
But forward, to the endless track.
With every step, we heal, we rise,
Underneath those vast, unbroken skies.
Never again shall we retreat,
For we are whole, and we are complete.
In every loss, a lesson gained,
In every storm, a heart unchained.

41. Our own World

This is our world, where stars ignite,
And oceans stretch to endless night.
Where mountains stand with quiet grace,
And every dawn a new embrace.
This is our world, both wild and free,
A canvas vast, for you and me.
With every tree, a story told,
In whispered winds, in sunsets bold.
Our world is made of hearts that soar,
Of laughter loud, and tears that pour.
It's in the rain, it's in the song,
In places where we both belong.
We share the sky, the earth, the sea,
Our spirits bound in unity.
In every struggle, we find our way,
A shared tomorrow from today.
This is our world, a fleeting dream,
A place where nothing's as it seems.
Yet in its depths, we rise and stand,
Together strong, hand in hand.

42. A heart of thanks

With every breath, I find my way,
In gratitude's light, I choose to stay.
For all the gifts the world provides,
For every moment, love abides.
For friends who lift me when I'm down,
For laughter shared, for smiles found,
For gentle hands that guide me near,
For all that's kind, for all that's dear.
For mornings bright, for sunsets warm,
For peace that follows through each storm,
For lessons learned and wisdom gained,
For joy that's lived and grief that wanes.
Gratitude fills my soul and mind,
In every corner, peace I find.
So in this heart, a song I sing,
A prayer of thanks to everything.
In the quiet moments, soft and still,
I pause to reflect, to feel and to will,
A heart that's full, a spirit light,
For all that's good, for all that's right.
The kindness given, the love I find,
The simple joys that fill my mind.
A smile, a word, a hand to hold,

These treasures more precious than silver or gold.
For the sun that rises, the stars that gleam,
For the hope that lingers, like a quiet dream.
For every blessing, small or grand,
I give my thanks with an open hand.
Gratitude flows like a gentle stream,
A reminder of all that life can mean.
In every moment, I choose to see,
The beauty around, the gift to be free.
So I lift my heart and say with grace,
Thank you, life, for this sacred space.

43. GRATITUDE

In moments quiet, calm, and bright,
I find my heart takes gentle flight.
Thankful for each step I take,
For every bond that love can make.
For simple joys, for skies so wide,
For those who walk close by my side.
For every dawn, for each soft night,
For stars that shimmer, pure and bright.
Gratitude in every breath I claim,
A quiet echo, soft and tame.
In small things, I see life's grace,
In every smile, a warm embrace.
Thank you, world, for all you give,
In gratitude, I choose to live.
I give thanks for the sun's warm glow,
For the gentle breeze that helps me grow.
For quiet moments, soft and clear,
For loved ones close, always near.
I thank the stars that fill the night,
For dreams that soar, for hope's pure light.
For kindness shared, both great and small,
For life's rich gifts that fill us all.

Each step I take, each word I say,
Gratitude guides me along the way.
For every blessing, seen or unseen,
I offer thanks, serene.

44. Guilty Pleasures

In quiet moments, when no one's near,
I indulge in things I hold most dear.
A piece of chocolate, rich and sweet,
A hidden book where worlds retreat.
I binge on shows, no judgment here,
Lost in a story, forgetting fear.
A lazy day, with no demands,
Just drifting through life with idle hands.
Music plays, though the lyrics might hide,
Secrets I keep, tucked deep inside.
A second helping, I can't resist,
A stolen hour, a stolen bliss.
These guilty pleasures, small and light,
Bring comfort in the quiet night.
Though the world may never see,
They're moments just for me, you see.
No harm is done, no pain or loss,
These fleeting joys, I pay the cost.
For in these things, I find release,
A fleeting taste of simple peace.
So let me have my quiet ways,
In these small pleasures, I'll spend my days.
For in their warmth, I'm free to be,

Myself, without a mask to see.

45. Treasures

In the heart of a forest where whispers reside,
Lie treasures unspoken, where secrets confide.
Glistening petals in the dawn's gentle light,
Hold stories of ages, in colors so bright.

Beneath ancient trees, where the soft shadows play,
Treasures of wisdom lie hidden away.
The rustle of leaves shares a tale from the past,
Of dreams that were woven, of moments held fast.

The warm, golden sunbeams dance on the stream,
Each ripple a treasure, each glance a new dream.
Nature's own vault, filled with laughter and grace,
Holds gems of the heart, in this sacred place.

The laughter of children, the song of the breeze,
Are treasures of spirits, that put the soul at ease.
A smile from a stranger, a hand that you hold,
In moments like these, the greatest treasures unfold.

So treasure the simple, the small acts of love,
For the richest of jewels come from the above.
In kindness, in beauty, in life's gentle mesh,
These are the treasures that truly refresh.

46. out of focus

In twilight's haze, the world begins to blur,
Where edges fade and colors softly mix,
Each thought a whisper caught in dusky air,
An atmosphere that lulls the mind to dream.

A single leaf, a shadow danced in light,
Unraveled soft, its crispness fades away,
Where clarity once ruled, now visions blend,
And all feels distant, like a fading song.

What once was sharp—the lines, the shapes we knew—
Now swirl in gentle chaos, calm yet strange,
A moment captured, yet just out of reach,
As time escapes, like sand that slips through hands.

The heart finds solace in this quiet drift,
A place where reason softens, giving way
To mysteries that shimmer in the dusk,
A world transformed, yet felt in tranquil peace.

In this unfocused gaze, we learn to see,
How beauty lies in all that's undefined,
For in the blur, the heart begins to grasp
The hidden truths that clarity might hide.

47. The ballad of the lost kingdom

In a land where the sunflowers sway,
And whispers of magic fill the air,
Once thrived a kingdom, bright as the day,
Where laughter danced, and hearts laid bare.

The princess, fair with a heart like gold,
Dreamed of quests and adventures untold,
But a shadow lurked, as the elders told,
A curse that made the night feel cold.

One fateful morn, with the dawn's first light,
She donned her cloak and sought the wood,
Through enchanted trees where day turned to night,
She wandered deep, as a hero would.

The fae folk sang, with voices clear,
Their laughter sparkled like starlit streams,
They spoke of a dragon, filling hearts with fear,
But the princess believed in her wildest dreams.

"Fear not," she said, "I'll seek out the beast,
For within its heart may lie the key,

To lift the curse, and restore the feast,
I'll free my people, and set them free! "

Through valleys deep and mountains high,
She ventured forth with courage true,
With every step, she heard the sky
Whisper secrets of wonders anew.

At last, she found the dragon's lair,
A cavern deep where shadows played,
Yet in its gaze, she found not despair,
But a soul trapped, in darkness frayed.

"Great beast," she spoke, in a voice so kind,
"I see your heart beneath scales so rough,
Together we'll weave a tale entwined,
For love is stronger than the fiercest stuff. "

With a gentle touch, she broke the spell,
The dragon transformed, its heart set free,
Together they flew, o'er the land they fell,
Bringing joy back to the kingdom's glee.

The curse was lifted, and cheers filled the air,
With the dragon as guardian, fierce yet wise,
The princess ruled with a heart laid bare,
In a kingdom bathed in endless skies.

So heed this tale of courage bold,
Where kindness blooms and hearts entwine,
In every story of magic retold,
A fairytale lives, where love will shine.

48. Emotions Personified

Joyful leaps, a sunbeam bright,
Overflowing, pure delight.
Yearning heart, a whispered plea.

Sorrow weeps, a silent tear,
Aching void, consumed by fear.
Deep despair, a shadowed tree.

Nervous fidgets, restless pace,
Eager hope, a smiling face.
Serenity, a tranquil sea.

Anger burns, a fiery brand,
Numbing shock, a trembling hand.
Grief's embrace, a chilling breeze.
Envy stings, a jealous freeze.
Resentment festers, slow and deep.

49. Legacy of Elara

A girl lived by Willow Creek's gentle flow,
With laughter bright, a sunlit, joyful glow.
Her name was Elara, a spirit free,
Whose mirth could charm the wildest, weary bee.
Her hair, like spun gold, danced in the breeze,
Her eyes, twin pools reflecting sunlit seas.

Her laughter echoed, a cascade of sound,
Through rustling leaves, on hallowed, fertile ground.
The birds would pause their songs to listen near,
The squirrels would peep, devoid of any fear.
Even the grumpy badger, old and gray,
Would pause his digging, and then steal away,
To listen, charmed, to Elara's glee,
A melody that set his spirit free.

But Elara's laughter held a deeper grace,
A mystery veiled upon her youthful face.
For in her heart, a sorrow softly slept,
A secret burden, carefully kept.
Her parents gone, lost to a fever's blight,
She lived alone, with only fading light
Of memories cherished, whispered in the night.

Yet still she laughed, a beacon shining bright.

Each morning dawned, she'd greet the rising sun,
Her laughter springing forth, before the day begun.
She'd gather wildflowers, petals soft and sweet,
And weave them garlands, tiny, vibrant treat.
She'd talk to rabbits, scampering in the grass,
And watch the river's currents gently pass.
She'd climb the willow, branches strong and high,
And sing her songs beneath the boundless sky.

One day, a traveler, weary and forlorn,
Came to the creek, his spirit quite withdrawn.
He'd journeyed far, through landscapes bleak and gray,
His heart was heavy, hope had slipped away.
He saw Elara, laughing by the stream,
A vision radiant, like a sunlit dream.
Her mirth surprised him, touched his wounded soul,
A healing balm, making him feel whole.

He sat and listened, as the sunlight played,
Upon her face, a masterpiece displayed.
He learned her story, of the loss she bore,
The quiet sorrow hidden deep at core.
He spoke of kindness, of the strength within,
To overcome the darkness, and to win.
He shared his wisdom, gleaned from years of strife,

And helped her find a purpose in her life.

Elara, touched by his compassion's art,
Found solace in his gentle, loving heart.
She learned to share her laughter, not just keep,
The joy contained, her sorrow buried deep.
She used her laughter, like a healing balm,
To soothe the wounded, to keep hearts from harm.
She helped the villagers, with cheerful grace,
And brought a smile to many a weary face.

The traveler stayed, and with each passing day,
Their bond grew stronger, in a special way.
He taught her skills, to help her live and thrive,
And showed her how to truly stay alive.
He helped her tend a garden, green and bright,
And filled her days with love and gentle light.
They built a cottage, nestled near the stream,
Where laughter echoed, like a joyful dream.

Years went by, and Elara's laughter rang,
A testament to joy, a vibrant song.
The villagers loved her, for her heart so kind,
A shining beacon, leaving none behind.
Her laughter filled the valley, far and wide,
A comforting solace, a joyous tide.

And though the sorrow lingered, soft and low,
Her laughter blossomed, helping all to grow.

One autumn eve, as twilight softly fell,
Elara's laughter echoed, a sweet farewell.
She passed away peacefully, in sleep's embrace,
Her life a testament to love and grace.
Her laughter's memory, a legacy untold,
A treasure precious, more than gems or gold.
And by Willow Creek, where willow branches weep,
Her laughter's echo lingers, soft and deep.

The villagers remember, year by year,
The laughing girl, dispelling every fear.
They plant new willows, by the flowing stream,
And whisper tales of Elara's joyful gleam.
Her laughter lives on, a spirit ever bright,
A testament to hope, a guiding light.
So let her laughter fill your heart today,
And chase away the shadows, come what may.

The legend speaks of Elara's gentle soul,
Whose laughter healed, making spirits whole.
And though she's gone, her legacy remains,
A whispered echo, in the sun and rains.
The laughing girl of Willow Creek's sweet sound,
Forever echoes, on hallowed, sacred ground.

50. The story of still water

The river whispers secrets, cold and deep,
Its surface mirroring the clouds above,
A shimmering expanse where shadows sleep,
Reflecting heavens in a silent love,
Each ripple a small story it does keep,
A timeless current, ever strong to shove.

The ocean roars, a boundless, hungry shove,
Its waves relentless, crashing on the deep,
A power ancient, that will never sleep,
Its salty breath, a constant, whispering love,
Where sun-drenched coral castles softly keep,
Their secrets hidden, in the currents above.

Far above, the rain clouds gather, love,
A gentle shower, or a furious shove,
Providing lifeblood, helping all to keep,
Their thirsty roots submerged within the deep,
A soothing balm, to soothe and gently shove,
A mirrored sky, reflecting all above.

The wellspring bubbles, pure and clear above,
A hidden source, where quiet waters sleep,

A life-giving spring, a tender, constant love,
A gentle push, a constant, gentle shove,
Protecting secrets that the earth will keep,
In its dark depths, a hidden, silent deep.

Down in the deep, where mysteries sleep,
A silent pressure, a relentless shove,
The ocean's heart, a bottomless, dark love,
Reflecting starlight, from the world above,
The wellspring's promise, that it will still keep,
A constant flow, that will forever move, shove.

The relentless shove, the constant, steady move,
A force of nature, where the secrets sleep,
Reflected in the waters, calm above,
A powerful current, that's given and will keep,
A timeless presence, a passionate love,
The mystery of depths, the endless, silent deep.

51. not sure where I am

The fog hangs heavy, a shroud of grey,
Across the moorland, where lost I stray.
No sunbeam pierces this chilling mist,
My path obscured, my bearings twist.

I woke this morn, in a slumber deep,
A dream dissolving, secrets to keep.
No memory stirs of where I've been,
A hollow echo, a world unseen.

The wind it whispers, a mournful sound,
Across the heather, barren ground.
A twisted oak, its branches bare,
Stands sentinel, in the misty air.

I clutch my cloak, a threadbare thing,
No comfort offers, no solace bring.
My throat is parched, my spirit low,
Where do I wander, where do I go?

A distant raven, its cry so stark,
Echoes my sorrow, leaving its mark.
A broken pathway, barely traced,

Leads through the shadows, a ghostly waste.

A crumbling stone, with carvings worn,
A nameless grave, where hope is torn.
A whispered legend, a forgotten tale,
Of wanderers lost, in this desolate vale.

The stars appear, a faint, cold gleam,
Reflected dimly, in a silent stream.
But offer no guidance, no light to see,
Only the vastness, surrounding me.

I call out loudly, a desperate plea,
But only silence answers to me.
My voice is swallowed, by the wind's despair,
Lost in this landscape, beyond compare.

Is this a purgatory, a shadowed place?
Or simply a wilderness, lost to time and space?
A punishment rendered, a life undone,
Or just a traveller, beneath the pale moon?

I stumble onward, with weary feet,
Through tangled brambles, bitter and sweet.
A fleeting glimpse, of a distant spire,
A fragile hope, igniting a fire.

Perhaps a village, a haven near,
Where friendly faces, will calm my fear.
A chance to remember, to find my way,
To shed this darkness, and greet the day.

But the fog descends, a chilling embrace,
Obscuring the spire, leaving no trace.
I am adrift, in this lonely plight,
Lost in the darkness, of endless night.

I am not sure where I am, I only know,
This haunting mystery, I must somehow bestow
Upon the world, a riddle untold,
A wanderer's journey, forever bold.

The mist still lingers, a ghostly veil,
As I press onward, my spirit frail.
I am not sure where I am, but I will find,
A way to break free, leave this place behind.
The path unclear, the future unknown,
Yet hope remains, a seed newly sown.
I journey on, through the misty grey,
Praying for dawn, and a brighter day.

52. Can you keep a secret ?

Can you keep a secret,
whispered in the folds of dusk,
where shadows curl like forgotten dreams,
and the night holds its breath?

A hush drapes the air,
soft as the sigh of a breeze,
as I confide in the stars,
tiny witnesses in their shimmering cloaks.

Here in the silence, a tapestry unfolds,
stitch by stitch,
each thread woven with tenderness,
stories tucked away in the heart's quietest corners.

Once, I glimpsed a moment,
a fleeting glance at what could be,
the fragile beauty
of possibilities untouched,
like petals in the morning dew,
still unturned,
still blissfully unaware.

Can you cradle this secret,
like a fragile bird,
against the cold of the world?
Hold it close,
let it warm in the light of trust,
for there is power in knowing,
and solace in the shared essence
of whispered truths.

In the vastness of existence,
these secrets mold our journeys,
tiny lanterns lighting the way,
reminding us we are never alone,
even in the deepest stillness.

So can you keep a secret?
In the garden of our thoughts,
let's plant this trust,
and watch it grow,
knowing some stories thrive
in the spaces where no one else hears.

53. I was meant to be there

In the quiet of the morning light,
When dawn begins to break,
I felt a whisper in my soul,
A path I had to take.

With every step, the world unfurled,
And dreams began to soar,
The echoes of a distant call,
Said, "You were made for more. "

Through valleys deep and mountains high,
Each twist led me anew,
In the heart of wild adventures,
I found a piece of truth.

I traveled through the whispering woods,
Where shadows danced and twirled,
And in the stillness, I could hear
The secrets of the world.

The laughter of a thousand hearts,
The stories yet untold,

Each moment stitched with golden thread,
In a tapestry of bold.

I wandered by a silver stream,
Where dreams and rivers flow,
And felt a surge of certainty,
That this was where to go.

For in each smile and gentle breeze,
In every songbird's flight,
I knew the stars had drawn me here,
To witness all the light.

So when the night is heavy and dark,
And shadows loom and fray,
I'll hold on tight to the belief
That I was meant to stay.

In the fabric of this journey bright,
I find my place, my care,
With every breath, I know it true:
I was meant to be there.

54. A Risk worth taking

In the quiet hum of the ordinary,
where comfort wraps like a thick blanket,
there lingers a whisper,
a pulse of something more,
calling from beyond the safe shore.

It beckons with a shimmer of possibility,
the promise of unraveling,
of stepping into the unknown
where paths twist like rivers,
and dreams stretch wide as the sky.

What if the compass points awry,
and the stars shudder in uncertainty?
Yet, amidst the doubt,
an ember ignites—a flicker, a dance,
the thrill of bending the rules of fate.

To leap is daunting,
with the unknown sighing at your heels,
but the familiar, though warm,
can become a cage of rusted bars—
static, silent, and suffocating.

So we take the leap,
armed with the courage of hope,
each heartbeat an echo of potential,
each breath a testament to the brave,
the wayfarers of uncharted realms.

For in the risk lies the discovery,
the uncovering of dreams
that would never dare bloom
in the shadows of the safe,
but flourish in the wild, open spaces.

And there, beneath the vast expanse,
we find ourselves,
not just surviving but thriving—
casting off the chains
and dancing with the stars,
knowing that every risk worth taking
is a story waiting to unfold.

55. oh! I don't remember it

It's hard to write a limerick, you see,
With a dream so elusive and free,
A half-remembered scene,
A fantastical queen,
And a landscape that's blurry to me.

There was moss, I recall, thick and green,
On a pathway where shadows convene,
With a twist and a turn,
As the sun did not burn,
But glowed with a soft, ethereal sheen.

A creature, a beast, I had seen,
With eyes that were emerald and keen,
It glided and flowed,
Its form softly showed,
A serpent of scales, yet serene.

This queen, clad in silver, I glean,
Her laughter, a musical stream,
She beckoned me near,

Whispered secrets I hear,
Or perhaps it was just a daydream.

A castle, it loomed, it would seem,
Built of bone and of moonlight's pale gleam,
Its towers so high,
Reached up to the sky,
Reflected in a translucent stream.

A feeling of peace, 'twas the theme,
A comfort, a mystical dream,
But now it's all gone,
Like the light of the dawn,
A half-remembered, forgotten extreme.

The path, and the queen, and the stream,
And the creature, all fading, it seems,
The castle so grand,
Lost in time's shifting sand,
Just fragments, a whisper, it teems.

A touch, a soft breeze, a faint gleam,
A memory's ghost, a fleeting beam,
The colours all blend,
As the dream starts to end,
Leaving only this fractured, vague scheme.

The moss, and the serpent, the queen,
This half-remembered scene, pristine,
A limerick's form,
Can't fully transform,
This feeling so poignant, unseen.

So I'm left with this sense, half-supreme,
Of a journey, a mystical dream,
A fragment, a trace,
Of time and of space,
A half-remembered, ethereal theme.

The limerick's rhythm, a strained, subtle plea,
To capture a dream that escaped from me,
Its fragments remain,
A whispered refrain,
A half-remembered mystery.

56. The passage of time

Like sand slipping through a restless hand,
Moments fade, like footprints in the sand.
Each second whispered, soft and swift,
A fleeting shadow, a gentle lift.
The days stretch long, then disappear,
A silent river, flowing near.
We chase the hours, but they slip away,
A dream unfolding, day by day.
What once seemed endless, now feels small,
The years rise up, then softly fall.
A glance, a touch, a memory's spark,
Leaves its mark, then drifts into the dark.
Yet in this dance of dusk and dawn,
We find ourselves and carry on.
For time, though fleeting, leaves behind,
A quiet beauty in the mind.
Each moment passed, a precious rhyme,
Etched upon the soul—the passage of time.

57. A Letter to Tomorrow

Dear Tomorrow,
I hope you're listening, though I don't know who you are,
A flicker of light on the edge of the horizon,
A whisper waiting to unfold—
Yet, here I am, speaking to you from today,
With all the questions and hopes that fill this moment's breath.
I wonder,
Will you be kinder than today?
Will you carry less weight in your hands,
Or will your sky still be heavy with uncertainty?
I've seen so many tomorrows,
Each one a promise half-kept,
Each one a door slightly ajar.
I'll send you my worries,
Tuck them in the folds of your sleeves,
But don't let them crush you—
Carry them lightly, as I hope to learn to do.
Will you bring peace, or will you bring change?
I'm learning to accept either.
I leave my dreams with you,
Wrapped in fragile paper,
Hoping you'll treat them gently.

They may not be perfect,
But they are mine,
And I trust that you will understand.
Tomorrow,
What will you bring me?
A sunrise I've never seen?
A world with a softer touch?
Or just another chance to begin again,
To pick up the pieces and start over?
I wait for you,
With all the courage I can muster today,
And all the hope I dare to carry
Into the arms of tomorrow.
With hope,
Today

58. footprints in the sand

One day, I walked along the shore,
The waves were crashing, hearts unsure,
The sun hung low, a golden strand,
And softly, footprints marked the sand.
I walked alone, with thoughts so deep,
Of memories I longed to keep,
Each step I took, a silent prayer,
A wish to find thc strcngth to caie.
But then I saw, with heart's dismay,
Two sets of prints, side by side, they lay.
At first, I thought that I had dreamed,
For in my mind, it only seemed,
That one set came from love's own hand,
And one was mine, alone, to stand.
Yet as I walked, the prints did fade,
With every step, they were delayed,
And soon I noticed, to my grief,
One set of marks was incomplete.
I stopped and turned, my heart in pain,
And saw the truth beneath the strain—
For as I walked, I came to know,
That the prints beside me, long ago,
Had not been mine, but his, so true,

A love that walked beside me, too.
But in my darkest times, I saw,
The second set, now gone, no more.
Where once his steps had stood so tall,
Now only mine remained to call.
And I cried out, "Where did you go?
Why, in my pain, were you not so
Beside me still, through storm and strife?
Why have you left me in this life?"
Then came a whisper, soft and kind,
That calmed my soul, and healed my mind.
“My child,” it said, “When you were weak,
And walked the road you couldn’t seek,
I carried you, though you couldn’t see,
For in your heart, you carried me."
The footprints, now, were plain and clear,
The truth emerged, and so sincere—
Through every trial, each test, each pain,
He walked beside me once again.
And though the storms may rage and roar,
I know now that I’ll walk no more,
Alone, for in the darkest night,
He’s there beside me, holding tight.
So when you see, in times of doubt,
That only one set prints about,
Know that you’re not walking alone—
For in your heart, you’re always home.

59. IN THE DREAM

In the dream, the air was thick with fire,
The sky ablaze with unspoken desire.
Darkness spun like threads of fate,
As I stood at the edge, too soon, too late.
The ground trembled beneath my feet,
Echoing the rhythm of a heart's deceit.
Figures rose from shadows long,
Their silent whispers an ancient song.
In the dream, I searched for truth,
But found only mirrors of my youth.
Every step led me further astray,
Chasing echoes that would not stay.
In the dream, the air was soft and clear,
A gentle calm that drew me near.
The trees whispered with voices kind,
As if to soothe my restless mind.
Paths of light stretched far and wide,
Leading me where mysteries collide.
The world around me hummed with grace,
Every moment in its perfect place.
In the dream, I felt no weight,
No burden, no need to hesitate.
With every step, the sky seemed bright,

Guiding me gently through the night.
In the dream, the world was painted gold,
Where moments bloomed, both young and old.
The air was warm, yet cool to touch,
A quiet peace that said so much.
Mountains rose with soft embrace,
While rivers whispered, tracing space.
I wandered freely, lost and found,
In a dream where silence held no bounds.
In the dream, there was no need to roam,
For every step was a step toward home.
A place of balance, calm, and light,
Where day and night were both in sight.
In the dream, the sky was painted blue,
A canvas vast, with endless hue.
The winds were soft, the earth stood still,
As if the world obeyed my will.
I walked through fields of whispering flowers,
Time slowed down, in gentle hours.
Each step I took, the ground would hum,
A melody of where I'd come.
In the dream, there was no race,
No hurry, no need to chase.
Just quiet moments, crisp and clear,
A peaceful world I held most dear.

60. A Letter to My Younger Self

Dear younger me, I see your fight,
In the quiet shadows, in the endless night.
You're searching for answers, for signs to guide,
But trust that the journey will help you find.
The road may twist, the path may bend,
But don't fear the roads that seem to end.
Each step you take, though unsure and slow,
Will lead you places you're yet to know.
You'll face your doubts, your heart may break,
But in those moments, you'll learn to wake.
The pain will pass, the sun will rise,
And in those storms, you'll find your prize.
Don't rush through life, don't hurry to grow,
There's beauty in moments you might not yet know.
Every tear you shed, every laugh you share,
Will weave a story beyond compare.
So trust yourself, as time unfolds,
For you are stronger than you've been told.
Hold on to hope, let go of fear,
For brighter days are drawing near.
With love from the future, you'll see in time,
Every step you took was part of the climb.

So keep dreaming, keep living, keep being true,
You've got this, dear one, and I'm proud of you.

61. BLUE

Blue, the color of the endless sky,
A deep, soft whisper that drifts on high.
It paints the ocean with quiet grace,
A tranquil mirror, a peaceful space.
In morning light, it softly wakes,
A promise in the dawn that breaks.
It holds the air, the breeze, the sound,
A gentle hue where dreams are found.
Blue is the calm in a stormy sea,
A cool embrace, a mystery.
It's the sapphire depth of midnight's kiss,
A quiet promise of pure bliss.
Blue runs through rivers, clear and wide,
A timeless current, a steady tide.
It holds the weight of far-off skies,
And in its gaze, the world defies.
The color of truth, so vast, so bold,
A hue of stories, yet untold.
It's the eyes of love, the heart of peace,
A silent song, a soft release.
In the pale blue of a winter's morn,
It holds the world, the earth reborn.
A calm reminder, in shades so true,

That everything fades—except the blue.
In every moment, in every sigh,
Blue reminds us of the reason why—
We search for solace, we seek the hue,
Of skies above, of oceans true.
So here's to blue, in all its grace,
A color that time cannot erase.
It's in the stars, the seas, the air—
A timeless love, forever there.

62. self - discovery

I wandered paths with doubts in hand,
Uncertain steps on shifting sand.
The world was vast, yet I felt small,
Searching for meaning, wanting it all.
I looked to others, seeking light,
In faces bright, in hearts so bright.
But still, the questions filled my mind,
Who am I? What will I find?
The road grew long, the shadows deep,
But in the stillness, I began to keep
The whispers of my own heart's song,
A voice that whispered, "You belong."
I found no map, no perfect way,
No guide to lead me through the day.
But in the silence, I learned to hear,
The truths I carried, held so near.
I am the sum of dreams and fears,
Of all the laughter, all the tears.
I am the lessons from the past,
The courage that I've learned to last.
Each day I see a little more,
A piece of me I hadn't explored.
The puzzle forming, bit by bit,

The parts of me I now commit.
In this discovery, I now stand,
Not lost, but holding my own hand.
For in the searching, I have found,
That I am whole, and I am unbound.

63. The art of creating

With brush in hand, I paint the sky,
Each color born from a silent cry.
A splash of blue, a streak of gold,
Unveiling stories yet untold.
In words, I weave a fleeting thought,
A piece of me that can't be bought.
Each line a thread, each verse a dream,
A quiet echo, a distant beam.
Music flows like rivers wide,
Notes that pulse with truth inside.
A chord, a beat, a voice that sings,
A melody that softly clings.
Through hands that mold, through hearts that burn,
Creation calls, and I return.
A dance of self, a whispered sound,
Where I am lost, and yet I'm found.
It's in the moments, raw and true,
Where every stroke, every word, feels new.
The act of creating is to be alive,
To give and take, to dream and strive.
From paint to words, from sound to form,
Each creation breaks the norm.
Through art, we live, through art, we see,

The endless ways we come to be.

64. The language of silence

In the space between each word,
A quiet truth is softly stirred.
Not all is spoken, not all is heard,
In silence, hearts can be inferred.
The gaze that lingers, soft and still,
Carries more than lips can spill.
In silence, we are bound and free,
A language of eternity.
The weight of hands that never part,
Speak volumes in the language of the heart.
No need for noise, no need for sound,
In silence, love is truly found.
A sigh, a pause, a gentle breath,
The silent plea before the death
Of words too small, too frail, to say,
What silence whispers in its way.
So let us speak with tender pause,
And listen closely to its cause,
For in the quiet, we shall see
The things we can't yet understand fully.

65. The Power Of Music

A note rises, a quiet hum,
A world of sound begins to come.
From strings that weave, to drums that call,
Music rises, filling all.
It speaks without a single word,
A language pure, yet rarely heard.
It dances through the heart and mind,
A rhythm deep, a pulse entwined.
A melody that heals the soul,
And makes the shattered parts feel whole.
It lifts us up when we are low,
A secret strength we cannot know.
Through every beat, through every tone,
We find the truth we call our own.
A song can break, a song can mend,
A faithful friend until the end.
It carries joy, it carries pain,
A fleeting moment, yet it remains.
In every ear, in every heart,
Music gives us the perfect start.
For in its power, we transcend
The world around us, and ascend.
A symphony of life's design,

The power of music, divine.

66. the garden of imagination

In a quiet room, with walls so gray,
A child sat dreaming the hours away.
With pencil in hand and paper near,
She painted worlds both far and clear.
Her room transformed with every stroke,
A kingdom rose, a mighty oak.
Dragons soared and castles gleamed,
As she wove the world of what she dreamed.
She painted skies of purple hue,
Where suns would rise, and stars would strew
A golden path to far-off lands,
Where oceans danced on silver sands.
A mountain grew beneath her gaze,
Its peaks were wrapped in morning haze.
She sailed on clouds, she soared on wings,
Through realms untouched by earthly things.
She crossed the seas with ocean blue,
To find a world where dreams come true.
A land where trees could sing and talk,
Where flowers grew with every walk.
She met the creatures of her mind,
And with them, she was free, unlined.

No limit here, no boundaries near,
Her imagination held no fear.
And though the world outside was still,
Her mind would race and dreams would fill
The quiet room, the silent space—
A universe she'd freely trace.
For in her mind, the worlds could grow,
Where all was possible, all could flow.
Imagination, bright and grand,
Would always be her guiding hand.
So, if you find the walls too tight,
Just close your eyes and take to flight.
For in your mind, you hold the key—
To all the worlds you wish to see.

Space For Your Thoughts

Space For Your Thoughts

Space For Your Thoughts

Space For Your Thoughts

Space For Your Thoughts

Space For Your Thoughts

(psst.. if this space isn't enough you can write in any other paper or just buy this book, it's much more convinient)

www.ingramcontent.com/pod-product-compliance
Lightning Source LLC
LaVergne TN
LVHW041106150826
845673LV00007B/1947

* 9 7 9 8 8 9 6 9 9 6 9 6 5 *